Properties of Materials

Smooth or Rough

Charlotte Guillain

www.heinemannlibrary.co.uk

Visit our website to find out more information about Heinemann Library books.

To order:

☎ Phone +44 (0) 1865 888066
🖷 Fax +44 (0) 1865 314091
🖳 Visit www.heinemannlibrary.co.uk

Edited by Charlotte Guillain and Catherine Veitch
Designed by Joanna Hinton-Malivoire
Picture research by Elizabeth Alexander
Originated by Heinemann Library
Printed by South China Printing Company Limited

ISBN 978 0 431 19349 6 (hardback)
13 12 11 10 09
10 9 8 7 6 5 4 3 2 1

British Library Cataloguing in Publication Data
Guillain, Charlotte
Smooth or rough. – (Properties of materials)
530.4'17
A full catalogue record for this book is available from the British Library.

Acknowledgements

The author and publishers are grateful to the following for permission to reproduce copyright material:
© Capstone Publishers p. **22** (Karon Dubke); Corbis pp. **14** (© Look Photography/Beateworks), **18** (© Simon Jarratt); Getty Images pp. **4** (Lyn Balzer and Tony Perkins/Taxi), **8** (Lauri Rotko/Gorilla Creative Images); Photolibrary pp. **11** (Dave Reede), **16** (Grady Reese/Fancy), **17** (Juice Images), **19** (Fancy); Shutterstock pp. **5** (© Jan Kranendonk), **6** (© Sherrianne Talon), **7** (© Serggavrilov), **9**, **23 middle** (© AJM), **10** (© grafvision), **12** (© rudiuk), **13** (© JCVStock), **15** (© Valentin Russanov), **20**, **23 bottom** (© matka_Wariatka), **21**, **23 top** (© Ana Cmelic).

Cover photograph of a boat reproduced with permission of Shutterstock (© Benjamin Howell). Back cover photograph of tree bark reproduced with permission of Shutterstock (© Valentin Russanov).

The publishers would like to thank Nancy Harris and Adriana Scalise for their assistance in the preparation of this book.

Every effort has been made to contact copyright holders of any material reproduced in this book. Any omissions will be rectified in subsequent printings if notice is given to the publisher.

Contents

Smooth materials

Some things are smooth.

Smooth things are flat.

Smooth things have no bumps.

Smooth things have no cracks.

Rough materials

Some things are rough.

Rough things are not flat.

Rough things can have bumps.

crack

Rough things can have cracks.

Smooth and rough materials

Glass can be smooth.

It can have no bumps.

Glass can be rough.
It can have bumps.

Wood can be smooth.

It can have no cracks.

Wood can be rough.
It can have cracks.

You can tell if something is smooth
or rough.

You can feel if something is smooth
or rough.

Smooth things feel flat.

Rough things feel bumpy.

Smooth things can look shiny.

Rough things can look dull.

Quiz

Which of these things are smooth?

Which of these things are rough?

Picture glossary

 **dull** not bright

 **rough** not smooth

 **shiny** bright

Index

Note to parents and teachers
Before reading
Tell children that smooth things are flat and have no bumps or cracks. Rough things are not flat and can have bumps or cracks. Ask children: "How do you know if something is smooth or rough?". Tell children the way to determine if an object is smooth or rough is by looking at objects and feeling objects.

After reading
Play a game of Guess what's in the box. Gather several shoe boxes, and place smooth and rough objects inside the boxes. Blindfold children or cut a medium size hole in the box lids. Get children to reach inside a box and feel the object. Children have to describe the object to a partner or small group and explain if it is smooth or rough. Once all the children have felt the object in a box, they can guess what the object is.